S0-BZO-863

THIS IS **MY** BOOK:

_____

CLASS OF: _____

GRADUATION

(FRIENDS FOREVER)

an autograph book

VITAMIN C

RUTLEDGE HILL PRESS®
Nashville, Tennessee

A THOMAS NELSON COMPANY

Copyright © 2001 by Colleen Fitzpatrick.

"Graduation (Friends Forever)" words and music by Colleen Fitzpatrick and Josh Deutsch
℗ 1999 Elektra Entertainment Group. All rights reserved.

"Graduation (Friends Forever)" by Colleen Fitzpatrick and Josh Deutsch
© 1999 Warner-Tamerlane Publishing Corp. BMI, Blanc E Music BMI, and Big Black Jacket Music BMI.
All rights administered by Warner-Tamerlane Publishing Corp. BMI.
All rights reserved. Used by permission. Warner Bros. Publications U.S., Inc., Miami, Florida 33014.

Photograph of Vitamin C on page 6 reprinted by permission of Elektra Entertainment Group.

Photographs on pages 12, 30, 35, 57, and 59 courtesy of University School of Nashville.
Photographs on pages 3, 8, 11, 33, 36, 38, 49, 63, 64, and front cover © Digital Vision Ltd.
Photographs on pages 5, 15, 16, 19, 20, 22, 23, 29, 52, 55, 56, front and back endsheets, and back cover
© Patrick Sheándell O'Carroll/PhotoAlto.
Photographs on pages 9, 13, 17, 21, 28, 31, 34, 39, 47, 51, 53, 54, 61, and 62 © Photodisc Inc.
Photographs on pages 4, 26, 40, 43, 44, 45, 46, 48, 50, 58, and 60 © RubberBall Productions.
Photograph on pages 25 © The Stock Market.

All rights reserved. Written permission must be secured from the publisher to use or
reproduce any part of this book, except for brief quotations in critical reviews and articles.

Published by Rutledge Hill Press, a Thomas Nelson Company,
P.O. Box 141000, Nashville, Tennessee 37214.

Cover and text design by Gore Studio, Inc.

ISBN: 1-55853-910-7

Printed in the United States of America
1 2 3 4 5 6 7 8 9 – 06 05 04 03 02 01

GRADUATION
(FRIENDS FOREVER)

Colleen Fitzpatrick and Josh Deutsch

SO WE TALKED ALL NIGHT about the rest of our lives,
Where we're gonna be when we turn 25.
I keep thinking times will never change,
Keep on thinking things will always be the same.
But when we leave this year we won't be coming back,
No more hanging out, 'cause we're on a different track.
And if you got something that you need to say,
You better say it right now
'Cause you don't have another day,
'Cause we're moving on and we can't slow down.
These memories are playing like a film without sound.
I keep thinking of that night in June.
I didn't know much of love but it came too soon.
And there was me and you and when we got real blue
We'd stay at home talking on the telephone.
We'd get so excited and we'd get so scared,
Laughing at ourselves thinking life's not fair.
And this is how it feels…
As we go on, we remember
All the times we had together.
And as our lives change,
Come whatever,
We will still be friends forever.

So if we get the big jobs and we make the big money,
When we look back at now will our jokes still be funny?
Will we still remember everything we learned in school?
Still be trying to break every single rule?
Will little brainy Bobby be the stockbroker man?
Will Heather find a job that won't interfere with her tan?
I keep—keep thinking that it's not good-bye,
Keep on thinking it's our time to fly.
And this is how it feels…
As we go on, we remember
All the times we had together.
And as our lives change,
Come whatever,
We will still be friends forever.

Will we think about tomorrow like we think about now?
Can we survive it out there?
Can we make it somehow?
I guess I thought that this would never end,
And suddenly it's like we're women and men.
Will the past be a shadow that will follow us around?
Will these memories fade when I leave this town?
I keep—keep thinking that it's not good-bye,
Keep on thinking it's our time to fly.
As we go on, we remember
All the times we had together.
And as our lives change,
Come whatever,
We will still be friends forever.

I wrote "Graduation (Friends Forever)" thinking about friendships in my own life. In high school, I always thought that I would be friends forever with the people who were important to me. This song was written after I had been out of school for a few years and realized how difficult it is to maintain a level of intimacy over time — but also, how important it is.

Graduation is really the first time we experience separation anxiety in our most important relationships. It is a time of conflicting emotions because one door closes while another opens to wonderful opportunities. It is a time of ambiguity. The future is full of possibility. Facing the unknown is both frightening and exciting. We ask ourselves, "Can we make it?" We realize the value of the friendships we are leaving behind. We trust that the power and strength of these friendships will keep us connected even as we move forward. Over and over, we will repeat this cycle in our lives. Doors will close and new doors will open. Graduation is often our first experience of that.

I have been surprised by how meaningful "Graduation (Friends Forever)" has been to people. Around the world, people have responded even more to the idea of friendship than to the idea of graduation. Friendship is one of the few experiences in life that transcends age, gender, sex, and culture. The song is for people looking back on what was and what could have been and, of course, for people looking forward to the future with great expectation. People have related the lyrics to significant transitions in their lives, from losing a friend, loved one, or family member to simply watching others move away. These memories will always be with us. Even after a person is gone, the friendship remains.

VITAMIN C

So we
TALKED
all night about
THE REST OF OUR LIVES,

WHERE
WE'RE
GONNA
BE
WHEN WE
TURN 25.

I keep thinking times
will never
CHANGE,

KEEP ON
THINKING
THINGS WILL
ALWAYS
BE THE

SAME

But when we leave this year

we won't be coming **BACK,**

No more hanging out 'cause
WE'RE ON A DIFFERENT **TRACK.**

AND IF YOU GOT **SOMETHING**

THAT YOU **NEED** TO SAY,

YOU BETTER SAY IT RIGHT NOW
'CAUSE YOU **DON'T** HAVE ANOTHER DAY,

'CAUSE WE'RE moving on

and we can't **slow down.**

THESE MEMORIES ARE

PLAYING

like a film
without SOUND.

I keep thinking of that night in June.

I DIDN'T KNOW
MUCH OF **LOVE**
BUT IT CAME
TOO
SOON.

And there was

ME

and

YOU

and when we got real

BLUE

We'd stay
at home talking
on the telephone.

WE'D GET SO **EXCITED**

AND WE'D GET SO **SCARED,**

LAUGHING

at ourselves thinking life's not *fair.*

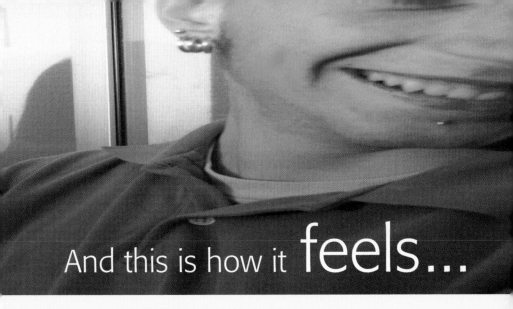

And this is how it feels...

As we go on, WE REMEMBER

All the times we

HAD TOGETHER.

AND

AS

OUR

LIVES

CHANGE,

Come WHATEVER,

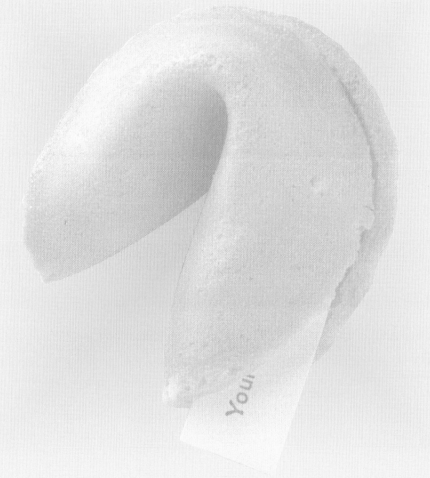

You

We will still be

FRIENDS FOREVER.

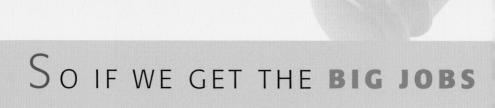

So if we get the **BIG JOBS**

AND WE MAKE THE **BIG MONEY,**

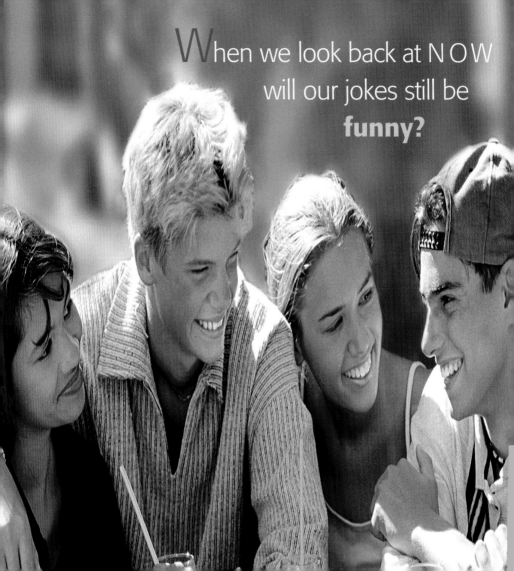

Will we still

REMEMBER

everything
we
learned
in
school?

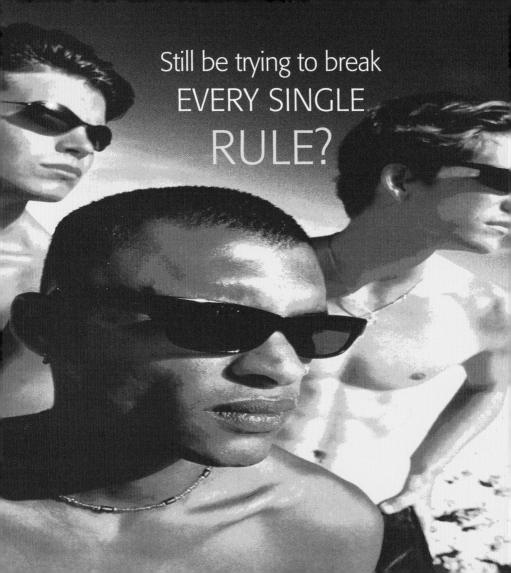

Still be trying to break
EVERY SINGLE
RULE?

Will little brainy Bobby be the stockbroker man?

Will Heather find a JOB
that won't interfere with her TAN?

I keep—

keep thinking
that it's

NOT

GOOD-BYE,

KEEP ON THINKING IT'S OUR TIME TO

FLY

And this is how it
feels...

As we go on, WE REMEMBER

All the times we HAD TOGETHER.

And as our
lives change,

COME **WHATEVER,**

We
will
STILL
BE

friends

FOREVER

Will we think about tomorrow
like we think about
now?

Can we survive it OUT THERE?

Can we make it SOMEHOW?

I guess I THOUGHT

And

SUDDENLY

it's like

we're

women

and

men.

that this
would
never
END,

Will the past be a shadow that will follow us around?

I keep—

keep thinking that it's not

good-bye,

Keep on thinking it's our time to fly.

AS WE GO ON,

WE REMEMBER

All the times we had

TOGETHER.

And as our lives change,

Come **WHATEVER,**

We will STILL be

FRIENDS FOREVER.